Usborne

First Sticker Book

Bugs

Illustrated by Marcella Grassi

You'll find all the stickers
at the back of the book.

Words by Caroline Young

Designed by Yasmin Faulkner

Bugs all around us

There are all kinds of amazing bugs to spot in gardens and parks. Add some stickers to see how many are flying, buzzing, crawling and slithering around these garden flowers.

In the jungle

Some of the biggest and most beautiful bugs in the world live in hot, steamy jungles. Stick some onto the pages to bring this jungle to life.

On the grasslands

Millions of bugs live alongside the lions, giraffes and elephants that roam the grasslands of Africa. Can you add some to this scene?

Lots of butterflies

Some butterflies are as big as your hand but others are as small as your fingernail. Fill these pages with fluttering butterflies of different sizes from all over the world.

Ceylon rose
butterfly

In the swamp

This swamp is home to masses of water-loving bugs. Fill this page with orb spiders, whirligig beetles and more.

In the desert

Bugs have to be tough to survive in the desert. Some, such as the antlion and the trapdoor spider, lurk in burrows waiting to pounce. Can you add some more bugs to this picture?

Massive bugs

The huge bugs on this page are shown at only about half their real size. Add stickers here to see some of the biggest bugs in the world.

Titan beetle

Queen Alexandra's birdwing

An Australian giant stick insect can grow to be as long as your arm.

Atlas moth

Goliath beetle

Scary bugs

Most bugs are harmless, but a few have poisonous bites and stings and should be left alone. Add stickers of some of these dangerous bugs here.

At 5.5cm (2in), the Asian giant hornet is as long as your finger.

Amazonian giant centipedes may grow to 30cm (12in) in length.

You could only just fit a giant weta from New Zealand in the palm of your hand.

Giant orb weaver spider

Fat-tailed scorpion

Bugs at night

At night, many bugs wake up and come out to look for food. Some of them even glow in the dark. Add some fireflies and glow-worms to this night-time picture.

Cabbage white butterflies

Red admiral butterflies

Common wasp

Honeybees

Bumblebee

Garden snail

Black ants

Dusky slug

Cabbage white caterpillar

Garden spiders

Seven-spot ladybirds

Aphids

In the jungle

Hercules beetle

Tarantula

Blue morpho butterflies

Scarab beetles

Jewel beetles

Golden scarab beetles

Painted weevils

Yellow crab spiders

On the grasslands

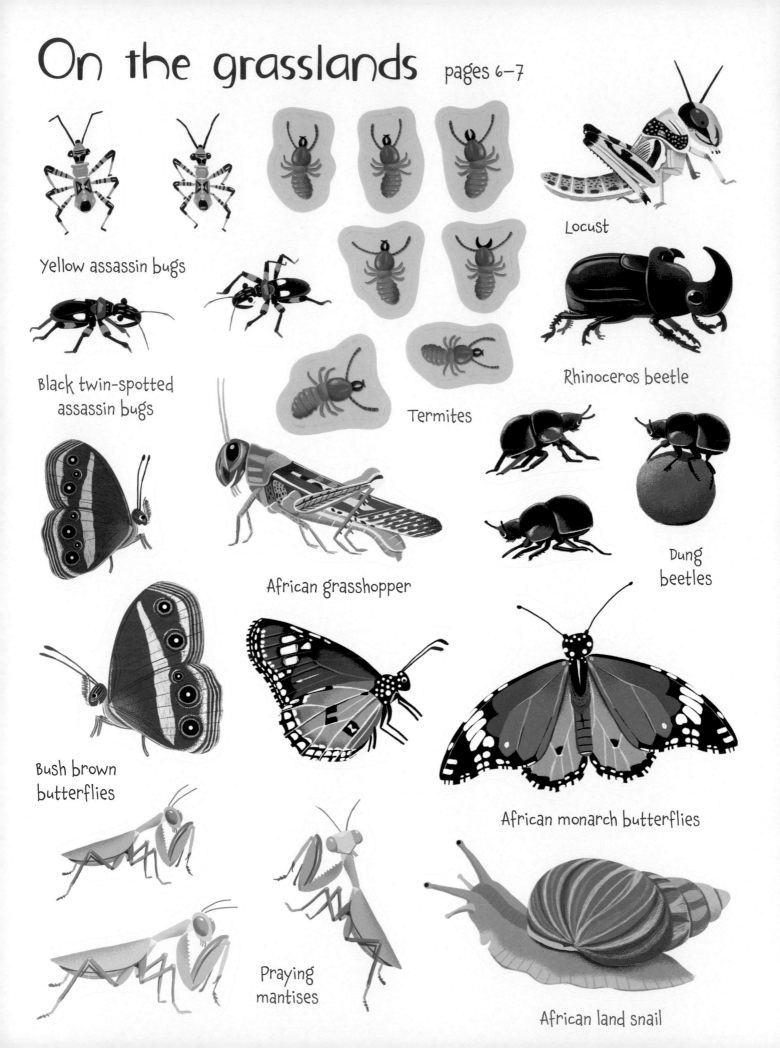

Yellow assassin bugs

Black twin-spotted assassin bugs

Termites

Locust

Rhinoceros beetle

Dung beetles

African grasshopper

Bush brown butterflies

African monarch butterflies

Praying mantises

African land snail

Lots of butterflies

Large tortoiseshell

Peacock butterfly

Clouded yellow

Common buckeye

Adonis blue

Purple emperor

Zebra swallowtail

Provençal fritillary

Western pygmy blue

Jamaican giant swallowtail

Owl butterfly

Glasswinged butterfly

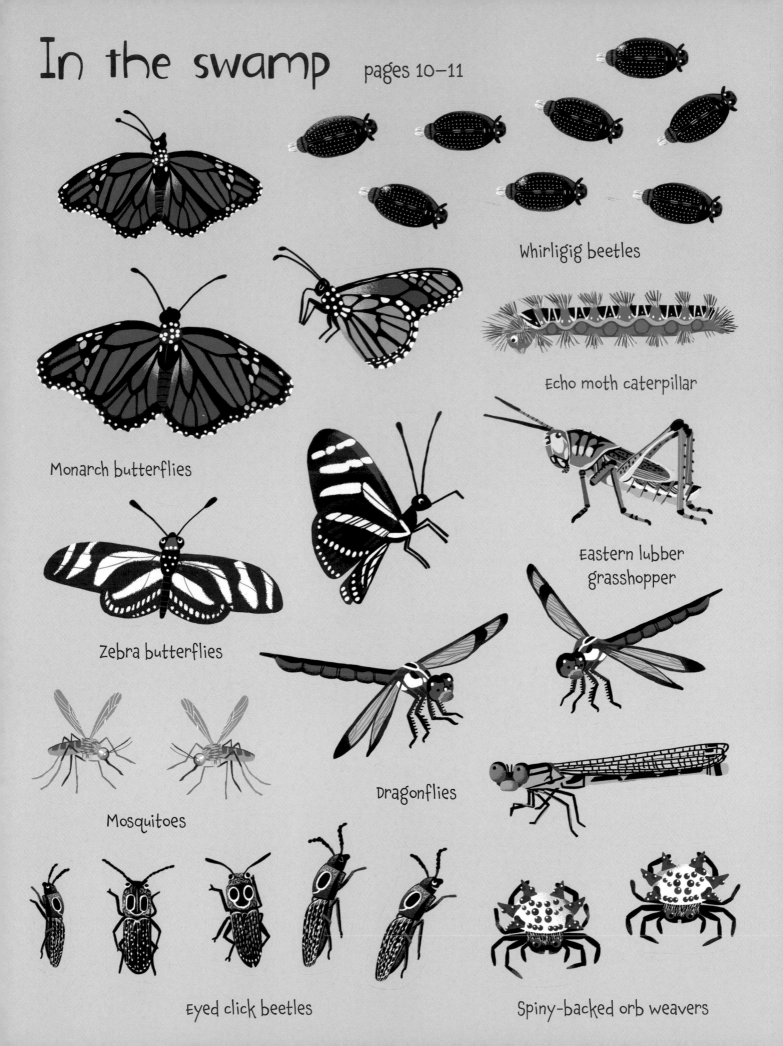

In the swamp

Whirligig beetles

Echo moth caterpillar

Monarch butterflies

Eastern lubber grasshopper

Zebra butterflies

Mosquitoes

Dragonflies

Eyed click beetles

Spiny-backed orb weavers

In the desert

Jewel wasps

Trapdoor spider

Western horse lubber grasshoppers

Scorpion

Scarab beetles

Antlions

Antlion larvae

Desert ants

Massive bugs

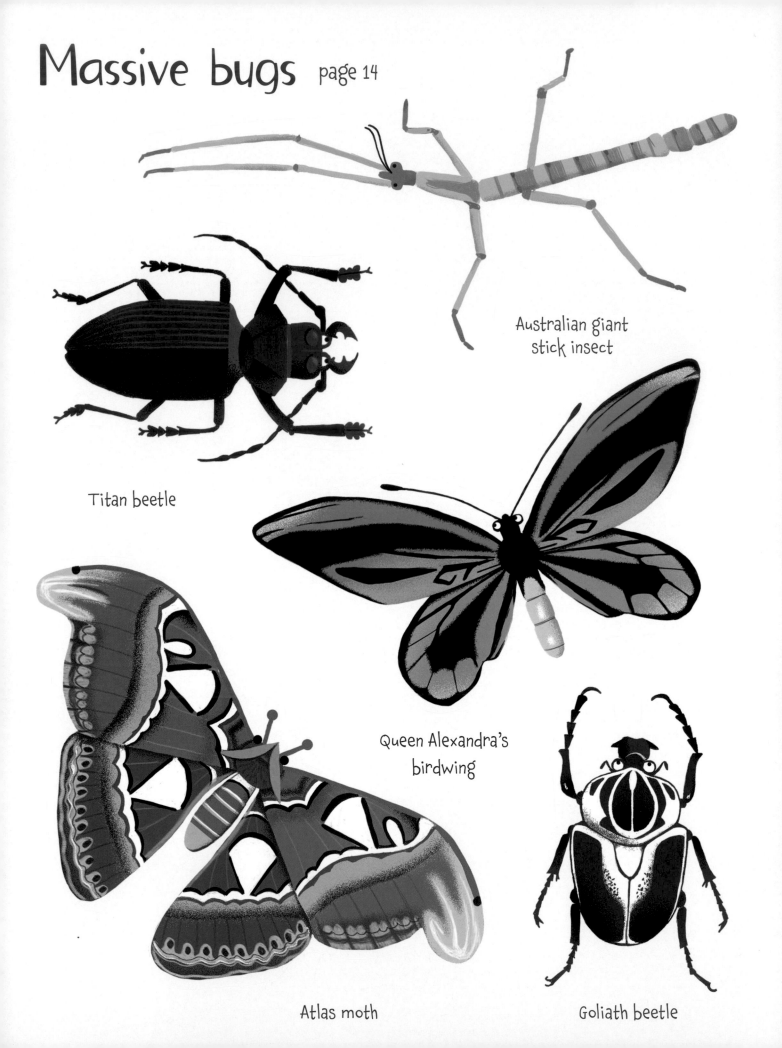

Australian giant
stick insect

Titan beetle

Queen Alexandra's
birdwing

Atlas moth

Goliath beetle

Scary bugs

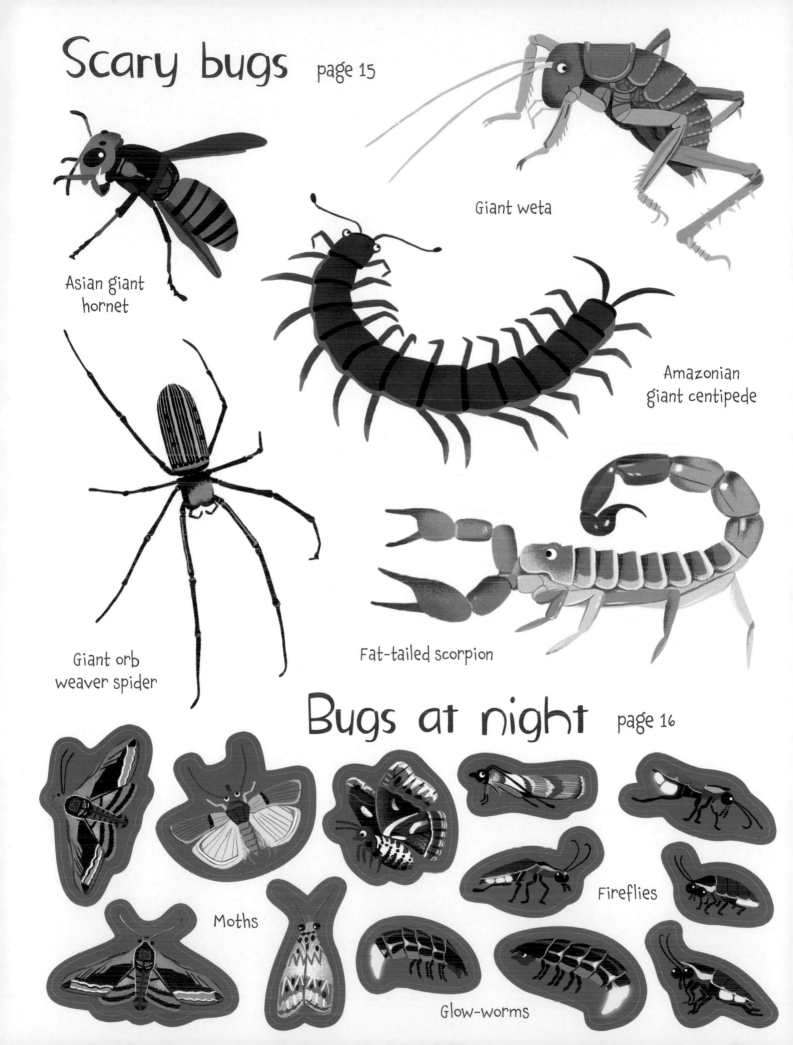

Giant weta

Asian giant
hornet

Amazonian
giant centipede

Fat-tailed scorpion

Giant orb
weaver spider

Bugs at night

Moths

Fireflies

Glow-worms